RICH HOFFMAN

SEDONA YOGI

SEDONA YOGI
Prescriptions From the Vedas and Medicine For the Mind
Richard Hoffman, Author

Copyright © 2020 Cities of Light Publishing
All Rights Reserved.

© Cover Art: Dreamstime
COVER and INTERIOR DESIGN: Yvonne Stepanow

No part of this book may be reproduced, reprinted, copied, or changed in any form without the written permission of the publisher or author.
The Divine Dichotomy: The Many in One is trademarked and protected by U.S. Trademark Laws. The Sedona Yogi is protected under The Divine Dichotomy copyright.

Published in the United States of America
by Cities of Light Publishing. Sedona, Arizona

Library of Congress
ISBN: 978-163625144B First Edition

CHAPTERS

---

1. DIVINE LAW — 16

2. MASTERY OF CHARACTER — 21

3. DIET: EVERYTHING IS ENERGY — 24

4. A SOURCE OF MANY — 35

5. CODE OF CONDUCT — 46

6. DIVINE DISCIPLINES — 56

Dedication

I have many teachers that I respectfully bow to and honor for their exemplary teachings.

My devotion and puja is dedicated to Sri Sathya Sai Baba, my guru.

Introduction

As a young boy of 6-years-old, I developed a relationship with Mother Earth, and she has been guiding me all along. In actuality, I was raised in a hair salon with hundreds of mothers. I like to joke that I may have been born on Mars, but I was raised by Venus who taught me the ways of the feminine energy-something I take great comfort in being around. I had cut hair for over twenty years, before I started writing this book. Thirty-seven years have passed behind the chair of cutting and styling, and importantly, listening and counseling the many who poured out their hearts to me with their joys and sorrows and intimate tales…These years of "consulting" with thousands of people have given me a certain insight into the human psyche!

My interests while growing up were music, astronomy, and the arts. My father was a hunter and my mother was a gardener. I loved the earth. I started meditating in my early twenties, but I didn't understand what I was doing until my thirties when I studied ancient wisdom and world religions.

I wrote and rewrote this book several times in my 30's and in my 40's while discovering and practicing Kriya Yoga. This is also the time in my life when I discovered my guru, Sri Sathya Sai Baba and the lotus of my heart opened.

I continue the practice of my yoga and I have come to understand that the writings of ancient religions and their wisdom teachings are here, even today, to remind us to guide us to maintain peace while in the midst of chaos; patience when there is aggravation; and love and understanding in place of fear. I now share these insights with my brothers and sisters to remind us of our divinity.

This book is my prayer and offering to Mother Earth.

The Golden Rule

Ancient Egyptian
"Do for one who may do for you, that you may cause him thus to do."

The Bahai World Faith
"Blessed is he who prefers his brother before himself."

Brahmanism
"This is the sum of Dharma (duty): Do naught unto others which would cause you pain, if done to you."

Buddhism
"A state that is not pleasing or delightful to me, how could I inflict that upon another?"

Christianity
"Therefore, all things whatsoever ye would that men should do to you, do ye even so to them for this is the law and the property."

Confucianism
"Do not impose on others what you yourself do not desire."

Hinduism
"This is the sum of duty: do not do to others what would cause pain if done to you."

Islam
"None of you (truly) believes until he wishes for his brother what he wishes for himself."

Jainism
"A man should wander about treating all creatures as he himself would be treated."

Judaism
"Thou shalt love thy neighbor as thyself."

Native American Spirituality
"All things are our relatives what we do to everything, we do to ourselves.
All is really One."

Roman Pagan Religion
"The law imprinted on the hearts of all men is to love the members of society as themselves."

Shinto
"The heart of the person before you are a mirror. See there your own reflection."

Sikhism

"Do not create enmity with anyone as God is within everyone."

Sufism

"The basis of Sufism is the consideration of the hearts and feelings of others. If you have not the will to gladden someone's heart, then at least beware lest you hurt someone's heart, for, on our path, no sin exists but this."

Taoism

"Regard your neighbors gain as your own gain, and your neighbor's loss as your own loss."

Unitarian

"We affirm and promote respect for the independence of all existence of which we are apart."

Wicca

"As long as you harm no one, do what thou wilt."

Yoruba

"One going to take a pointed stick to pinch a baby bird should first try it on himself to feel how it hurts."

Zoroastrianism

"Whatever is disagreeable to yourself, do not do unto others."

Dear Reader,

My intention in writing this book is to bring us together, though I know that the subjects discussed in these pages might be controversial and could create division among us. However, I ask you to dissolve any of your prior judgments and keep an open mind. Words can be very tricky; a single word may be interpreted differently by any number of people. I will share with you what some of the words here mean to me so that we are all on the same page.

This book is an introduction to the Love and Wisdom passed on for centuries by the many masters, teachers, and realized souls that have taught through example. My idea was to create a simple book that could be easily shared. Most books are surmised in the last chapter and this book is comprised of the sum of many chapters.

Wisdom — Intelligence — Spiritual

Wisdom is more than intelligence. Intelligence is more like the ability of the brain to process information. Wisdom is knowing the proper way to use intelligence for the good of all. The term "spiritual" is often misunderstood. Its root word, spirit describes the divinity or life force within every form. Therefore, spiritual refers to a person or ideas relating to the "light within" — the main ingredient of all life.

I intend to inspire you to study the great spiritual wisdom of many religions, belief systems, and people from all over the world and share it. This book contains the ancient wisdom of the Vedas of India and also the contemporary wisdom of sages and saints from the 19th-20th centuries.

On Listening...

The great sage Meher Baba came to America in the 1950s. This prophet had taken a vow of silence in 1925 and became well-known as the "silent prophet." This vow of silence created quite a stir in America. When asked by the many searchers (seekers), "What do you bring us?" Meher Baba would point to a letter board, which he used to create sentences, and then messaged: It's all been said! So, he said very little. He let it be known, you won't listen so, I won't talk. This is no doubt a divine joke from the Heavens for this same message has been put forth for thousands of years; yet, we still don't listen and continue to search.

Divinity...

It is not enough for an individual to undertake the study of material, moral, or even spiritual teachings. Reading and discussing the vast topic of what is Divinity is only the beginning of the process. Until there is committed action in one's daily life there are only words and speculation. To experience real Divinity, we must act Divine. Our soul's greatest desire is to express the divine in all our conscious actions. God has many interpretations and this book includes all of them. I believe God is everything and everywhere. God is life. Therefore, God is both form and formlessness.

Grace

Grace is a gift or reward not only to one who is full of grace or virtuous but also, as a challenge to those who need to see their greed or selfishness by not receiving what they desire. Therefore, grace is the "like attracts like" of the energy paradigm, or "As you sow so shall you reap." Grace like God is omnipresent and present in all of us.

Divine Love

Divinity or the divine is sacred and holy. These terms are used throughout the book to describe that which is truth, right action, and all that is positive in the Creation.

The word "Love" has many meanings. However, when it is used in this book I speak of devotional and selfless love. This love is unconditional and without expectation. Religion like spirituality is misinterpreted and misrepresented. All the world's religions are teaching the same basic values and stress honoring all beliefs as long as they serve God. Religion should not be blamed for creating divisions; the misinterpretation of their words and sacred scripture has divided us. All religions offer a path to divinity.

Prayers, mantras, and chants are all actions for affirming your intentions. These actions are exercises that strengthen sacredness in our mind and discipline us to right action.

Saint, sage, or lord are titles given to those who have mastered their thoughts, words, and actions. We remember their names and their lives, as shining examples for our liberation.

Consciousness

Consciousness is a word used throughout this book to describe the act of being aware of the self and all things outside of it. Being conscious is not only about the self but about all beings and all life.

Yoga can be simply defined as exercise. Yoga is designed to discipline the mind and body on the path to mastery.

This time that we find ourselves in is without a doubt a time of chaos that has been foretold in many scriptures and books of wisdom. I have included in this book ways for the transformation and cleansing of impurities especially good for turbulent times. This prescription of spiritual exercises is taken from the Vedas, the most ancient of the known scriptures from India.

It has been said that a 'master of love' proves his/

her mastery by loving not only those who are loving but also those who are hateful. It is easy to love those who are kind. The ultimate test of love is to love all—unconditionally. Someone who is a 'master of love' can speak the language of the listener. His speech reflects a loving heart. All religions, faiths, and creeds have many ways to honor, love, and respect all life.

Discipline, simplicity, and being true to the divine spirit are necessities in self-mastery. Also, there must be an understanding of unity consciousness and being a part of the collective oneness of all life. It will take many of us to join together in the unified field to achieve unity. But the process begins deep within the self.

Much love and many blessings to you on your Path to Mastery!

1
Divine Law

In the absence of that which you are not, that which you are, is not.

This may sound a little confusing; however, this is the Law of the Divine Dichotomy. We must remember that throughout creation we have opposites. Let's think about that. Everything electrical has both a positive and a negative charge and each opposite cannot function without the other.

We have light and darkness, good and bad, cold and hot. All of these could not be described without the experience of both extremes. We surely wouldn't be able to call something hot without experiencing cold. This is the dichotomy. That brings us to the "divine" part. I look at it this way: All life on this Earth is all made up of the same extremes of energy.

Our small individual worlds exist in a 'micro' sense, as a microsphere, whereas, the collective world and all its inhabitants make up the macro sense, the macrosphere. Both micro and macro-worlds affect and interact with one another. Add to this the great sun, the moon, the planets, and the stars and you are just an atom in the great body of the seen and the unseen universe of energy.

What is God?

Energy is the main ingredient of the Universe, right down to every single atom in your body. I believe that this life force energy is God.

> *God is oneness, love, life force, great spirit –*
> *everything and everywhere.*
> *If God is everything, then God has separated into a*
> *Divine Dichotomy to allow the experience*
> *of both extremes.*

Both a man and a woman are children of God and very different from one another. Man is strong and woman is gentle; man is analytical, and woman is nurturing. Look at the Yin and Yang symbol. It represents the Divine Dichotomy. Man and woman, electric and magnetic, white and black…However, most people didn't know that the two teardrop shapes of white and black are spinning. The symbol is captured in a still picture to show the dichotomy. But when the symbol spins, the separation of the two sides blend into a grey composite of the opposite colors, and thus, balances the dichotomy.

The question is: Are we blending or are we separating? I believe this is the task of our quest. When we are blending there is peace and love; however, when we are not blending, we create the division of opposites through separation. Therefore, we have the dichotomies of love and hate, happy and angry, good and bad. I'm sure all of us have felt the difference between these feelings and would choose to be happy, good, and loving rather than angry, bad, and full of hate. Maybe this is the game that we have created. But we do have the choice of free will to decide whether we want to experience "oneness" or "separation" within this Divine Dichotomy.

What does it mean to be separate? Separate from what?

If "oneness" is goodness, cooperation, love, and even God, is separation the opposite of God? Separateness values being separate more than being part of the whole. This is another part of the ego game whose main characteristic is creating separation.

What is this ego?

One of the aspects of the self is the ego. The ego of a highly developed individuality like Jesus was one of divine oneness. He taught us that we are all children of God. Everyone is your brother and your sister. The ego is very challenged by this perspective. The ego is competitive and treats others as if they're on the other team.

Have We Forgotten the Golden Rule?

Jesus is an example of a remarkable spiritual being at one with God. He taught us to treat others as we would want to be treated. This is one of the best ways to overcome the ego. If we treat others with disrespect or harm them then we have forgotten Jesus' advice. He teaches the truth of the maxim: *As you sow, so shall you reap.* Speaking ill of others with angry and hurtful words feels awful whether you're the one being spoken to or about.

Would polluting our world for energy be considered greedy and lacking in consciousness?

Is it greedy to fill our garbage dumps with more waste than we know what to do with? How can we possibly continue actions like these?

Dislike is also an example of ego addiction because the mind has decided that this situation is not how it likes it. Discontent shows the addiction about not being happy with something. The ego is addicted to the self and its only purpose is to please one's self interest. Talk about a drug… and a controlling one at that.

When we act involuntarily in a rage, it's a sure sign of our addicted ego- mind. If we are easily angered when situations are not as we want them to be, and we need to be always pleased, then we must look more deeply at our motives. Pointing fingers at others and blaming them for upsetting us, is only our ego saying that *I'm addicted or prefer to be around only those people who agree with me and won't challenge my opinions and lifestyle.* It is our own selves that cannot remain calm when we come face-to-face with situations that challenge our egos.

The ego is so powerful and controlling that it affects our families too, which affects our communities, our countries, and our world as a whole. We must make an effort to control the ego to change our selfish actions. This is the first exercise in this book. Selfish action is responsible for disharmony in ourselves and our world. In the microsphere of our minds, or in the macrosphere of collective consciousness, we create our world with our thoughts, words, and actions.

The mind and ego can be controlled. This has been proven by many people all over the planet. Many have shown how to calm the mind to master emotions and character. I challenge the reader to give it a try, and honestly look into your true Self. Like any addiction, the first step is to recognize it and then to have the will to change it. You will be amazed with the results, if you make an honest effort…one thought at a time.

Chapter One describes mastery of the ego in the best way that I know. I'm sure you have some descriptions of your own. I have presented the actions of the ego and the separation it causes to inspire you to understand this powerful energy that we call thought. The following chapters will share with you the wisdom that I have learned from others who express understanding of this energy that we call life.

2

Mastery of Character

Mastering the mind is not a two-week class with a certification. It's tough work and may bring many challenges to the surface before there is success. Please don't let this discourage you, because it's well worth the effort. I have been working on this challenge for over twenty years and I'm not done. However, I have made great improvements in my character and enjoy myself and my world much more now. Everyone will have their own path and ways to work on themselves. Some will have a harder struggle with this challenge than others. Some of us will understand this is easier than other disciplines that require self-mastery. I repeat, don't let your ego talk you out of the discipline required for the mastery. It will try many times. I know it will because I have stumbled many times on my path.

The first step to understanding your ego is simply watching yourself daily as your ego acts and reacts to the situations which you will encounter. This exercise will help you to recognize your ego addictions. If it helps, you could make a diary or log of the daily situations that challenge you. I start the day with a prayer to help me focus and affirm my plan for self-mastery and my intention to do it every day.

A prayer can be a wonderful affirmation for the self.

For example:

Let there be goodness in my eyes so that I may see the goodness in all things. Let there be understanding in my ears so that I may hear with humility. Let there be love in my mouth that I may speak sweetly. Let there be care in my hands that I may help and serve others."

You can reprogram the mind with a prayer like this one. At the end of the day look back at your encounters and ask yourself if you were able to act accordingly. If not, write down what challenged you or think about why you couldn't maintain a calm disposition without judgment. This will help you recognize your addictions and understand what it is you need to work on. An excellent way to end the day is to look at the challenges you had and replay them in your head, also replay them the way you could have acted according to your prayer. After you have completed this exercise, you should ask for forgiveness, if needed, for anyone you may have acted violent, cruel, selfish, short, or judgmental toward.

This will help you reprogram your mind and begin again

with humility. In instances when you have been harmful to someone or distressed him or her, it may be required of you to create forgiveness face-to-face. End your day with another prayer thanking the world for your challenges because they bring you closer to your higher self by understanding the ego addictions.

Eventually, you will use the above prayer for those challenging moments throughout the day, instead of just at the beginning of the day. This prayer helps to immediately align your mind and actions.

There are a lot of great books out there that can also be of service to reprograming the mind and creating affirmations for the self. Books can be a great distraction from the illusionary world that we tend to get caught up in and which fuels the ego and its desires. T.V., newspapers, violent music, and gossip are a few of the things we should cut out of our daily routine. This stimulation is ego food. My T.V. only comes on when I rent a movie and I don't rent violence or bloodshed. Like good books there are also great movies to uplift the soul and are great soul food. Remember we live in a world of dichotomy here and it is our choice what we decide to plug into.

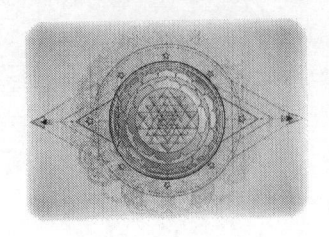

3

Diet: Everything is Energy

Everything is energy and has a character of consequence. A great book written by Eveline and Michio Kushi (1926-2014), titled the *Macrobiotic Diet* suggests that everything that you see, hear, taste, smell, and feel is influencing your emotions and health. All energy and its influences are received through your senses. Once the energy is received and interpreted by the mind, our body absorbs it. In other words, all your senses have to be regulated and are part of your ego's diet. We can reprogram the mind by disciplining the way we spend our day. It won't take long before you realize you didn't need some of those old habits anyway.

We need to slow things down a little bit so we're not so anxious. We need to calm the mind to have a better understanding of who we are and how we're expressing ourselves. This exercise is known as *self-realization*.

Let's talk about putting goodness in our eyes (seeing goodness). If we see that we are all God's children in search of our higher selves and that some of us are lost in our ego perspective, we might be able to see our brothers and sisters with more compassion. With this humility, we see the oneness in all creation and know that we are a part of this creation. By seeing goodness everywhere, we see that there is a need for being calm and peaceful to become a living example of goodness.

This perspective is true service and subtracts judgment from the mind. Goodness in our eyes is seeing the oneness in our world and treating all with honor and respect. All of us are God with his life force residing in each one of us.

Understanding in our ears is the understanding that some souls are still speaking with their egos and are going to talk selfishly or judgmentally. If we allow another ego to influence us and respond with the same energy, we have only multiplied this energy. We become the very thing that we judged in the first place.

Remaining calm with the understanding that not everyone has mastered his or her speech is the best posture and shows your mastery over what is heard.

Love in your mouth is the mastery of speech. Every word describes who you are and what you are creating. Speaking sweetly is a sure sign of a caring soul. People are very attracted to this kind of behavior and usually respond with sweetness in return. They can't help but love the beauty of love. Speaking sweetly will also influence the bliss within us as we enjoy the sweet harmony of our song. Speaking with love creates peace, and it is a great example to others, as well as pure service for all that listen.

Care in our hands would never hurt or harm another through physical violence or negative gestures. Care in our hands means just that, to care for another who needs help. This becomes a service to humanity through your work in society or any situation you encounter in your community. Service to others is a powerful exercise to eliminate our ego and its selfish needs. It has been said that hands that care are more powerful than lips that pray, for prayer is only the beginning of creation from the mind to the mouth, and hands that care is the action of love.

To summarize this chapter is to say we need to change our routine of selfish behavior or ego, into the right action that is selfless. This can also be described as being moral or having a virtuous character. Living a moral life is the essential first step in reducing egoism. Knowing is half the battle when incorrect or selfish action is recognized as the source of all pain. Although we may be burned repeatedly, some of us continue to reach into the fire.

Jonathan Roof's book, *Pathways to God*, says it best: "Morality is the adherence to truth, love, goodness, duty, peace, and nonviolence. These are the human values that are the core teachings of the world's religions. Maintaining high moral standards demonstrates our recognition of the divinity in others and ourselves. It shows our respect and consideration for others in thought, word, and deed. Right conduct is a function of our conscience, the voice within. The pursuit of a moral life is an unfolding journey, which takes us toward the God within."

This search is our true reason for living and we fulfill this duty when we value virtue rather than material possessions. In other words, to reach divinity we must act divine; this is the action of your prayers. We must become the grace that we are praying for and evolve into our higher selves. This has been the teaching of the saints and sages for centuries.

Science has confirmed that the building blocks of life are the atoms, and these are mainly made up of electromagnetic energy or virtual photons. Therefore, all material whether liquid, gas, solid, animal, plant, human, or mineral are made of atoms filled with light energy. Let me share with you a wonderful explanation given by Lawrence W. Fagg, a professor of nuclear physics and a holder of a master's degree in Religion. He writes in his book, *Magnetism and the Divine*:

"The great majority of space occupied by all earthly objects is impregnated with an astronomical number of such essential non-material phenomena in a constant flurry of activity. All things that appear to be solid or liquid or to have substance consist principally of this vibrant space. This can be understood by considering for example, a carbon atom in your pencil where some 99.97% of its mass is concentrated in the nucleus at its center, which occupies roughly one-trillionth of the volume of the atom as a whole. The remainder of the volume is occupied by six electrons (of very low mass) and trillions of virtual photons that transmit the electromagnetic force that keeps them in their orbits. Hence, we and all material earthly objects are a part of a vast ocean of essentially non-material space. Energized by an innumerable multitude of virtual electrodynamic phenomena."

Draw a circle and in the very center put a very small dot. This dot is the nucleus of the atom. Anywhere in the rest of the circle put six smaller dots; these represent the six electrons in a carbon atom. The rest of the circle is filled with trillions of virtual photons or electromagnetic energy.

Photon is the scientific name for light energy. Every building block of all matter that is known to man, or what we call the atom, is mainly made of light energy. This energy is not new news, we have known and tapped this energy right out of the air since the mid 1900's. I believe this energy is made up of information that creates the form or character of the matter. Just like when more atoms combine, they create cells and when cells combine, they make organs. Could light energy be like a thought? A thought can be described like a lightning storm in the brain with light traveling across neurons, creating different patterns with each thought. Maybe vibrations (or vibes as we tend to call them) move or ripple out from our bodies as we think and influence the chemistry of our atmosphere.

Professor Lawrence described it as "a vast ocean energized by an innumerable multitude of virtual electrodynamic phenomena." Deepak Chopra, M.D., also agrees that the mind is not just the brain but is composed of every cell. Experiments have been conducted in the hospital where patients healed faster when they were given comedy to watch. This is because when you are laughing or in a positive mindset, the whole body is listening and reflecting the thought. Every atom is a flashing light of information from every thought, influenced by the senses and the energy information that we receive with them. Our health and well-being depend on not only the food we eat but also the sights we see, the sounds we hear, the emotions we feel and the thoughts we think. Everything is energy and has a force of character. Why would it be said that a picture is worth a thousand words? A simple picture can create many thoughts and feelings that could spark a negative or positive reaction. The same is true for sound. What a powerful energy sound is, not only in music but in speech as well. Think about how music can change your mood. Also, what is said and how something is said can make a great impact. Words have tremendous power; they can calm or arouse our emotions, they direct, explain, or confuse. Music is an amazing potent force of energy. Music can influence the listener to tear with joy or aggressively dance.

I believe that we are constantly vibrating energy, and that every person is vibrating to their frequency, which is influenced by what they are thinking, saying, and being.

These vibes can be felt. I'm sure anyone of us could share a story about our experiences. Some might call it a "gut feeling," while others call it "intuition," but we have all experienced vibes. Energy is everywhere, and in everything for it is the force within every form and every atom. This would explain how some 'intuitives' who work for the police department can find out about a person from an article of clothing or even an object touched by that person. An energetic imprint or a fingerprint of information is in the photons and very sensitive people can feel it. Are we in a divine dichotomy of light and thought, interacting with one another creating formulas of energy? Action and reaction are the law of the universe. When we better understand the nature of energy, we will create it more wisely.

In many ancient belief systems, still believed today, energy is called by different names. The Chinese call it *Chi*; the Japanese call its *Qi*; Hindus call it *Prana*; native Hawaiians call it *Mana*. Is this energy or life force God?

Energy is taken in by all our senses and influences our emotions and behaviors. Therefore, sense control is the first step to controlling the influential energies that exist in some of our activities. By controlling the senses, we are referring to controlling our "macrobiotic diet."

This diet consists of everything we see, hear, taste, smell, and feel. The senses are literally our world. We receive all information with them and process it through our brain, which then decides what is seen, heard, tasted, etc. Our diet should not only be used to control our environment like what to eat, too listen and to watch. Our diet also consists of our behavior. If we allow our responses to be harsh, short, angry, etc., we become the very thing we would rather not see, hear, or feel. We become the very energy we have chosen not to ingest in our diet. Our diet becomes successful when we discipline our activity and how we respond to activities outside ourselves.

Eventually, as we control our senses, we will be able to control our thoughts and emotions. The discipline required in maintaining your "macrobiotic diet" will take time. However, a very important part of our spiritual exercises is centered on the ego and addictions — the very source of our separation and the reason for illnesses and complications.

I have yet to discuss food. This energy that we ingest three times a day, or more, is influencing your chemistry big time. Food and drink will influence how you feel as well as your health right now and only multiplies by the decades, as we age. I urge you to study the latest studies in nutrition and health. Sad to say, you won't find them at the doctor's office; they are busy selling medications.

Try health food stores, the library, the Internet, etc. You will be surprised to find out what a protein is and where you get them. I have been a vegetarian off and on for over twenty years now and would like to share with you some of the facts that I have learned through my studies and experiences over the past years.

The first thing that I'm asked when people find out is *where do you get your protein?* This fear of not getting enough protein is a great misconception in our society.

Books that I've studied, written by well-accredited doctors and nutritionists, tell us that we should eat foods with high protein content for energy.

Yet, there are hundreds of proteins and yet only a portion of them are not abundantly made by the body. Therefore, we have 22 amino acids that we call a "whole protein" that should be eaten.

Animal protein (cow, chicken, fish, pig, etc.) have only 18 of these amino acids and they take more energy from the body to extract their energy potential. Also, be aware that when you eat animal protein, the fat, hormones, and the diet of that animal gets introduced into your chemistry. Vegetable protein sources like avocados, spinach, and beets have all 22 amino acids and create more energy than they take to break them down.

However, the real news here is this: *Once you cook your food, the enzymes are destroyed.* The food becomes difficult to assimilate and anything left for the body to absorb as energy isn't much. In other words, proteins are made up of amino acids and amino acids are made up of enzymes. Enzymes are destroyed when we cook our food, and therefore, destroy the structure of the protein. With this in mind, are we really getting protein at all from our cooked food?

How much energy really is in our cooked food?

If everything is energy, then all food and drink are energies which are ingested daily affect the body accordingly. Proteins are not the most important ingredients in the diet, it's enzymes. Enzymes are very important, as without them you won't digest your food correctly, which means you won't assimilate your vitamins and minerals as well.

Enzymes are also very important to keep the blood oxygenated. Enzymes are abundant in raw food. They are heat sensitive, so the more we cook our food the more enzymes are lost... Guess what these enzymes are? Enzyme is another word for life force. Our body craves energy, and enzymes are magic for our health and nutrition. We think our body craves certain tastes and textures, but these are addictions of the mind and the tongue. Enzymes are what the body craves to stay healthy and full of the energy that feeds the blood, tissue, and cell growth.

I encourage you to study for yourself the truth about the energy in the food that we eat and how our digestive system works. The pH. of our chemistry is vital knowledge. Food and drink have a large impact on emotions and health. We need to use discipline in our diet and maximize the energy that we can acquire through what we ingest.

Collective Consciousness

I spoke earlier about the power of collective consciousness. What is collective consciousness? If most of humanity is stuck in their egos does that influence our world? Does this collective influence you? It takes great discipline to turn our eyes and ears away from the constant stimulation of materialism.

Sights and sounds are always tempting us to buy and partake in activities that bombard our senses. We must consider the price we pay when our lives become addicted to the very world that is killing us. We, as a collective, are very powerful and do amazing things every day. Consciousness is a very powerful energy within every person and especially within millions of people. We are all working together to create our world as we know it. We all buy food, fuel, and goods that generate their production, but at what cost? In the quiet of your mind, your conscience, what do you think? Our life is more than our next meal or our next pleasure. *I truly believe that life is for solving the mystery of the ego and its addictions. Life is about realizing who you really are. Life is about the oneness that we all are.* Life is the collective life force where we all interact together in the electrodynamic phenomena.

The Yin and the Yang, the male and the female, the electric and the magnetic. The Divine Dichotomy and the Many in the One.

4
The Source of Many

This chapter is dedicated to my teachers- past and present. These pages retain some of my original notes, which I took when I began this wonderful journey within myself.

> *"The best you can give this world is a healthy wonderful You!"*

This is my favorite quote (above) from the wisdom of Sri Sathya Sai Baba... The Buddha said, "We judge as if we were perfect, "meaning that the best teacher is one who is *being* what they teach.

Other important teachers who have had a big influence on me are Mahatma Gandhi who said, "It is nonviolence when we can love those who hate us." Also, Saint Francis who prayed for faith when there was doubt and for joy when there was sorrow.

St Francis' prayer asked for the best in our character. When we start with ourselves, we are ultimately serving others. Jesus Christ said, "Do unto others as you would have done unto you."

Love is our grandest expression and is what we want the most. Imagine sharing, honesty, and caring for all those you encounter daily. Every day you will see your lessons in your acceptance or non-acceptance of this idea. Any time that we find it difficult to be honest, reflect inward and contemplate, why? What are you afraid of? Are you willing to face it? Face your fears, understand them and realize there is nothing to be afraid of. We have all been taught these fears for generations. Most of us have the same ones, don't feel that you are the only one working this out. "There is nothing to fear but fear itself." As a child, my father wouldn't allow me to use the word 'can't' because when you do, you surely will not.

"Just let go, "is a wonderful mantra from brother, Forest. Let go of your past and the ritual of your ego. Making mistakes is how we realize we must do it differently next time. If we continue to make the same pattern of mistakes, we experience the same conclusions. If you continue to do what you have always done, you're going to get what you've always got. Certain actions and reactions have become habitual or involuntary.

When we act unconsciously, we are losing our integrity. Holding on to what we know is fear of the unknown.

But what about faith?

A belief is valueless if you don't test it and live by it. Belief converted into experience becomes faith. Until a concept becomes experience it is only speculation. Neal Donald Walsch wrote one of my favorite books, *Conversations with God*.

Neal Donald Walsch states: "Fear is the energy which contracts, closes down, draws in, runs, hides, hoards, and harms. Love is the energy that expands, opens up, sends out, stays, reveals, shares, and heals. Fear clings to and clutches all that we have. Love gives all that we have away. Fear holds close, love holds dear, fear grasps, love lets go."

I applaud Carolyn Myss, Ph.D., a medical intuitive. She is a wonderful source of knowledge. The first time I heard the *Energy Anatomy* tapes I was so excited to hear them, over and over. She has written many books and given talks on *why people don't heal and how they can*. She discusses the insights on how we block our own energy by holding onto past programs and painful experiences. She explains that these thoughts of the past are also affecting us now by just remembering them. This is life force spent on past experiences instead of on today's desires.

Another wonderful book, written by Elia Wise, titled *A Letter to Earth has this to say*: "One who is preoccupied with yesterday's experience is not available to be informed by today's universe. Being current with yourself is the posture of enlightenment." Elia also writes, "An enlightened being is one who fully knows their self, your embrace of life, your expression of love, and your aspiration to self-realization are essential to the circulation system of all that is. This is life feeding itself." This is a great book to be enjoyed and shared with many. I had visions of reading this book before it came to me. I imagine Elia as a wise woman, living in the forest with her young daughter. I felt as if a goddess of wisdom was talking directly to me and I was captured by her knowledge.

As I continue to gather information from many religions and belief systems, I realize that "Oneness" is taught by all religions. The word "religion" contains the prefix re, which means doing something again. The other part of the word connotes unifying. Religion may thus be interpreted as re-union. All religions are a path to Divinity. It has been our misinterpretation or misrepresentation of different religions that have caused separation. One who is not tolerant or respectful of another's religion is not a true follower of one's own religion or belief system. Pope John Paul II said, "Ut unim sint," or "That they may be one!"

Many discussions arise while you meet others studying the same subjects in the same circles. I met a dear friend, Tim, whom I remember walking in the Ponderosa forests of Northern Arizona and discussing 'selfishness.'

I remember mentioning how recognizing selfishness and the judgment we have toward selfishness was becoming more and more undesirable for me. He added that to recognize selfishness is in and of itself selfish. We concluded that when we judge another who acts for themselves only, we too become selfish in our judgement. The difference between judgment and observance is that judgment comes with conviction and observance can enjoy the difference. Celebrate the diversity and know we are one and not the same.

Sri Sathya Sai Baba said: "Love lives by giving and forgiving; Self lives by getting and forgetting. Love is selflessness; Selfishness is lovelessness."

St. Francis said: "You can't honor both money and God!" "Greed and lust are the downfalls of humanity."

I believe that what St. Francis means is that you can't honor both money and God if money is used for power or greedy ends. When it is used for good in the world then it is akin to God. Good money could be described as the blood of society.

Sai Baba said: "Every day whatever work you may be doing, do it in the name of God and make your life sacred. You should not think that worldly life and spiritual life are distinct. Do not make such distinctions like spiritual life is sugar and worldly life is tasteless water. You have to stir the water in the glass and let the sugar at the bottom dissolve well and then enjoy drinking the sweet mixture. In this way, worldly life should be blended and harmonized with spiritual life."

I have come to realize that it is more difficult to unlearn than to learn in life. Loving is easy, it's the fears that are difficult. The school of life is inside you. Our best lessons come from situations that challenge our perspectives.

The only challenge is in our mind because everyone will have their perspective on any different subject. Keeping a calm disposition shows that you have learned to master yourself.

Mastering the self is the intention of self-realization. Self-realization is to understand who you are and realize how you are expressing this knowledge of self. This practice of balancing the thoughts, emotions, words and actions is called Yoga.

The Vedas are ancient wisdom texts written thousands of years before Christ. Yoga was born from the Vedas. *Yoga means union.* A yogi (male) or yogini (female) are students on the path of self-realization or self-mastery. The goal of yoga is to calm the mind so that without interruption you may hear the wisdom of your higher self. These spiritual practices known as yoga include many aspects or techniques, more than the commonly known exercises of physical postures or asanas. There are also songs, chants, prayers, breath control, and meditation.

However, the most revered yoga exercise is called *bhakti* or devotion to God through service to mankind and all life. Everyone is your brother and sister. No two come together for the benefit of one. We are all teachers and students in this school of life. In our Divine Dichotomy, we are one and many-together. The expression "salaam" in Islam means the *merging of the many in one.* The Mayan saying: "In-lak'ech" means *I am another yourself. Advaita* is from the ancient Sanskrit language. It means *All is One.*

Yesu (Jesus) or Essu as he was called in other religious texts is used to describe Christ. This term "Christ" also signifies the oneness of divinity. The inner significance of the term "Yesu" is the recognition of the one divine in all beings.

> *"We are all Gods and children of the most high,"*
> *(Psalms 82:6)*

Jesus is found in many scriptures of the East and there are many stories about his own self-realization. Early on his path of understanding, he declared "I Am of The Light," and "I Am the Son of God." He later said, "I Am in The Light," or "God Is in Me." Jesus came to realize that he was even more than that, and declared "I Am the Light," or "I Am God." "I and My Father Are One." Jesus taught us that we too could grow into Divinity.

To love God is to love all as God. Meher Baba said, "If we understand and feel that the greatest act of devotion and worship to God is not to hurt or harm any beings, we are loving God." Overcome evil by good, sorrow by joy, cruelty by kindness, and ignorance by wisdom. Serve humanity as one's self. The highest thought is always that thought which contains joy. The clearest words are those words that contain truth. The grandest feeling is love. Realize you are one with God, and God exists equally and impartially in all beings. Then you will be able to love others, as your own self.

"The art of peace is to fulfill that which is lacking. "This quote is taken from the Master Morihei Ueshiba. His story is amazing and can be read in the book The Art of Peace, translated by John Stevens. Peace is art and it is the ingredient lacking in chaos. We must share our wisdom to grow our collective consciousness. Elia Wise writes, "Human consciousness is the capacity to focus, direct, and make meaningful the self-awareness of being." A balance of health, wisdom, and spiritual joy creates a successful life especially when we share these benefits with others.

Paramahansa Yogananda

A very wise swami (teacher) came to America from India in the early 1900s named Yogananda. He was loved all over the nation, and the world, for his lectures on peace, love, and the ways of Jesus and other saints and sages who professed the same. He founded the Self-Realization Fellowship in the nineteen twenties. His autobiography entitled, *Autobiography of a Yogi*, tells us of his amazing life growing up in India and meeting many God-realized souls all over the world. He truly shared the Love of God with so many. He writes that when he was a young man, his Guru Swami Sri Yukteswar asked him why he disliked organizational duties.

Paramahansa Yogananda said that he saw them as "hornet's nests." Sri Yukteswar corrected him and said, "Or, like hives, we are the bees and God is the honey. Are you going to keep the honey to yourself?"

This not only inspired Paramahansa to spread the message of Love and the honey of God to many, it also inspired me. I fell in love with this beautiful story and would remember a formula Paramahansa suggested after finishing the book and looking for another.

Paramahansa Yogananda said: "If you read for one hour, you should contemplate for two, and write for three." I interpreted this to mean, if all you are is someone else's books and thoughts, who are you? This ran through my mind at the bookstore as if Paramahansa said it to me. I was inspired to write the *Divine Dichotomy* that day. Now that I have experienced this formula through writing down my thoughts, I recommend it for you.

I continue to study and share my understanding every day. I mentioned at the beginning of this book that I am dedicated to evolving consciousness and feel empowered to be an example of a teacher ever growing. I know that sharing this wisdom is of my highest service and I invite any seekers of truth to contact me. For me, Bhakti Yoga is service to God and the many forms of this Creation. I end this chapter with a prayer.

Thank You, Great Spirit, the Mother, and the Father of the Universe for I am grateful for your love and desire nothing else.

God is Love, Lover, and Beloved.

Om Sai Ram.

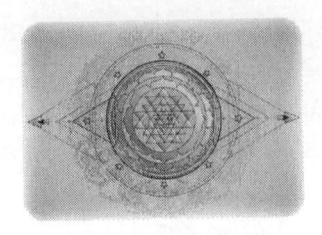

5

Code of Conduct

The Vedas are a most ancient series of religious texts written in Sanskrit, originating in ancient India. They are divinely revealed words written in stanzas that convey wisdom about the nature of God and human beings. The word *veda* is derived from the Sanskrit root or *vid*, meaning knowledge or wisdom. The Vedas impart a framework of knowledge that show us how to live, a code of conduct. The wisdom of the Vedas breathes pure and eternal truth as revealed by God through saints and sages. For thousands of years the teachings passed from mouth to mouth before being written at least three thousand years before Christ. However, much of the understanding of their wisdom has been lost over time.

The great sage, Vyasa, recognized the need to classify and collect the remaining Vedas for the benefit of future generations. He gathered and collated the teachings into four collections that still survive today. Vyasa also composed the Puranas and the Mahabharata and gave humanity the Bhagavata.

The four Vedas are the *Rig Veda*, the *Yajur Veda*, the *Sama Veda*, and the *Atharva Veda*. The *Rig Veda* is considered to contain the oldest material of the four Vedas and includes prayers and hymns to God for the realization and the understandings of life. The Yajur Veda elaborates the importance of dedicated acts to the Glory of God.

These promote the peace and prosperity of the world as that is the primary aim of all the Vedas. The Sama Veda includes the understandings of *sacred sounds* and their proper pronunciation.

In Sanskrit the *sa* signifies voice and *ama* signifies life; therefore, the combination of voice and life is the meaning of the word *sama*. The Atharva Veda gives the wisdom of preserving health and security of body and community. The Atharva Veda speculates on the origins and nature of humanity and God and leans toward the philosophical teachings of the Upanishads and Puranas. An excellent introduction to the Vedas is offered by A. Parthasarathy in his book the *Vedanta Treatise*.

From the Vedas, yoga was born and has been handed down and multiplied in various styles and lineages. I have learned Kriya Yoga exercises that I can simplify into five groups. The first group is called *Hatha Yoga* and is the practice of postures or asanas, mudras, and bandahs. Asanas refer to a posture that produces relaxation. A mudra is a gesture, movement, or position that affects the flow of pranic energy in the body. A bandah is a psychomuscular energy lock that redirects the flow of pranic energy in the body.

These exercises keep the body fluid and free of any energy blockages and increase the flow of prana energy. A person who has not had the benefit of the physical practice of yoga is in for a treat. Yoga is well known by athletes who want the benefits of keeping the body flexible through various stretching techniques.

Our second group of exercises is called *Pranayama* or the art of mastering the breath. Breathing is an important bridge between the mind and the body and can influence both of them. In the *18 Siddha Kriya Yoga Tradition* by Babaji, Marshal Govindan says: "Our breathing patterns reflect our emotional and mental states. The breath is jerky during anger, momentarily ceases during periods of fear, gasps during amazement, chokes during sadness, sighs in relief, and is slow and steady during periods of concentration. While it is difficult to control the mind and emotions directly, they can be mastered indirectly by using breath." Various meditation traditions have taught to concentrate on breathing smoothly in order to eliminate distracting thought. Deep breaths bring in more oxygen and oxygen is full of electromagnetic energy or prana and life force. Govindan writes, "As oxygen is taken up by the circulatory system, so is prana taken up by the nervous system and is spent as nerve-force and also magnetizes the iron in the system and produces the Aura as a natural emanation."

The third group of exercises is named *Dhyana Yoga* and

is art of mastering the mind through concentration, contemplation, and visualization or commonly known as meditation. Eventually the unruly mind is tamed of its repressed desires, fears, and memories or judgements and can calm itself into blissful silence to listen to the subtle vibrations of God.

Mantra Yoga is our fourth group of exercises and includes the sacred sounds used in prayers, mantras, chants, and songs to God. The name of God holds great power, whether remembered silently or chanted out loud. In Christian, Hindu, and other religious traditions, the creation is described as originating from sound or the word of God. Christians began to practice the repetition of the name of Jesus, nineteen years after his crucifixion. This practice not only distracts the mind from selfish tendencies but is full of Divine energy that is absorbed by the mind and body.

Shakti

The creative energy from which all things are born is known in Sanskrit as *shakti*. It is also known as Mother. Shakti or divine creative energy is all around us. This electromagnetic force creates and destroys according to the Universal Law of action and reaction. The process of creation is expressed in thought, word, and deed. If done for the good of creation, representing the compassion and love of Mother, then you create 'shakti' with a positive creative force. Of course, there is a dichotomy; you may choose the alternative and summon Kali, the Destroyer.

We are discovering the power of shakti in science, and

authors and artists. Dr. Masaru Emoto conducted many experiments with water that changed our world. He wrote several books on how water is affected by human interaction; one is entitled *Hidden Messages in Water*. Dr. Emoto describes how he experimented with the saying of both positive or negative words and phrases to water samples, and then, photographed their frozen crystal molecules to reveal amazing images. The water responded with beautiful designs and geometry when something positive was spoken, especially words of love and gratitude. However, when something negative was spoken the water responded with obscure and bland-looking splotches, clearly restructuring itself to the vibration it took on. This is proof of the power of 'shakti.' I encourage you to see the pictures for yourself in Dr. Emoto's books.

A brilliant artist named Alex Grey paints amazing art that details our energy fields and anatomy. A lot of his work can be seen in his book *Sacred Mirrors*. I have his DVD entitled *ARTmind*, which not only shows much of this but also has some of the philosophy behind this art. Alex Grey, a gifted visionary, shows us the unseen spiritual energy that composes our energetic matrix. His work is a must-see and an excellent aid for your imagery of Divinity.

Powerful energy is emitted from our bodies, minds, and speech. We should be very careful about what we think and say. Intent of good or bad plays a role in what is created and will influence our world. When in prayer or when singing devotional songs, this energy is doing its highest good. This is the power of prayer and why we say *grace* over our food before consuming it. Many people have had experiences of divine grace when sincerely praying. On the other hand, I'm sure all of us have experienced the opposite when we were careless with our thoughts and words. Thoughts and words have great power and should be treated with respect.

Bhakti Yoga

Our fifth group of exercises is called *Bhakti Yoga*. Vedic sages have described the 9 Ways of Devotion to God and these are considered paths of attainment and liberation.

They are:

- Sravanam (Listening to God's Glories)

- Keerthanam (Singing the Glories of God)

- Vishnusmaranam (Ever remembering the Lord)

- Paadasevanam (Worshipping the Lord's Feet)

- Archanam (Offering Daily Worship)

- Vandanam (Prostration)

- Daasyam (Dedicated Service)

- Sneham (Friendliness)

- Atmanivedanam (Total Surrender).

The particular form of God that one worships is less important than one's sincere devotion to the Divine.

Sri Sathya Sai Baba said: "The essence of Bhakti is love and not the formal exercises in japa."

Japas

Japas are sung or spoken mantras in which there is a repetition of the divine names. Worship should be offered to the Divine who resides in all beings. Love is God, {so} live in love. Love is the means of realizing the bliss of the self, which is centered in ourselves. It need not be sought elsewhere. It can be found within one's self when all thoughts are controlled, and the mind is turned inwards. Dedicate all actions to the Lord. This is the highest knowledge. It is the summum bonum of existence. Love should become a way of life. That alone is true devotion." As we discover that God resides in each one of us, God takes on many forms and is the force behind them all. Therefore, true Bhakti is your right action in all endeavors and becomes your devotion and service to God and all life. Bhakti is your smile, your helping hands, your sweet speech, your patience, and your loving thoughts.

*A sacred utterance, a numinous sound, a syllable, word or phonemes, or group of words in Sanskrit believed by practitioners to have psychological and/or spiritual powers. - Wikipedia

Bhakti is about loving and serving All.

Yugas

The most amazing information I discovered in the Vedas were the great ages of time or the Yugas. The scriptures speak of 4 Yugas, each lasting many thousands of years. The beginning of time is called Sathya Yuga, next came Tretha Yuga. The third is called the Dwapara Yuga, and now we are at the end of the Kali Yuga, the fourth.

"The Cycle of the Yugas within the ancient Vedic literature points to earth 'ages' that span vast periods. The Yugas reoccur time and time again and bring in definite stages of human development and form an integral part in the blueprint of human consciousness. Swami Sri Yukteswar, a Vedic scholar of tremendous note, discussed the ages of the yugas in his book The Holy Science, written in 1894. Sri Yukteswar is best known in the West as the guru of Paramahansa Yogananda (1893-1952), his primary disciple, who upon first seeing his prophesied teacher exclaimed, "Gurudeva!" Yogananda went on to found the Self-Realization Fellowship (SRF) in America, authoring the classic, *Autobiography of a Yogi* in 1946. He is acclaimed as the bringer of the discipline of yoga to America."

However, the great adepts have always said that spiritual advancement can be realized by focusing one's attention on illumination, a day-to-day quest for peace, compassion, and understanding of our fellow humanity, regardless of the Yuga that we are living in.

Have we been playing with fire? We have been warned not to participate in wrong action in all scriptures from around the world. We have created destruction in our formula of poor choices and attracted this wrath of Kali. In this current age of spiritual decline, the simplest means of liberation and redemption is through the remembrance of the name of God. This is the prescription for the Kali Yuga, whereas in other ages practices of strict behaviors where needed.

Winning God's grace in the past demanded tremendous discipline and effort. Perhaps attracting God's grace today requires less effort when so few people strive for virtue or liberation.

> *"In the beginning was the word and the word was with God, and the word was God."*
> *(Gospel of John, 1:1)*

Repeating your beloved Lord's name is powerful Shakti. Every cell in your body will vibrate this Divine creative power. There are many names to choose from and any name will do. Rama, Krishna, Buddha, Allah, Mother Mary, Jesus Christ, Jehovah, Yahweh, etc... Words have tremendous power. They can arouse emotions and they can calm them. They direct, they infuriate, they reveal, they confuse; they are potent forces that bring up great reserves of strength, wisdom, and feelings. Through Namasmarana the mind is gradually liberated from all its distracting thoughts, desires, and imagery, giving free play to the senses. Where the name of God is sung, there God is. Once you take on the name of the Lord that is sweetness itself, it will awaken all the sweetness latent in you. You will create an energy or a formula of heaven on earth that will protect and transform your fate in this

Kali Yuga. God's name should be said with devotion and sweetness without desire or reward. This mantra, prayer, or song is love and gratitude with contentment and praise.

Today all elements of the world are polluted. The sounds you hear are impure, as well as the actions you see. The air we breathe, foods and water that we consume are all losing their purity. The Kali Yuga has become the age of impurity. Namasmarana is a cleansing exercise to transform the negative thoughts, words, and actions that have polluted our consciousness, within, as well as in the collective. These sacred sound waves will permeate your world and purify it first, then influence others.

Every word becomes your mantra, so speak love. Every thought becomes your creation, think love. All action becomes your Dharma or right action when you are being love. Everyday whatever work that you may be doing, do it in the name of God and make your life sacred. Begin to realize who you are and watch yourself express your reality. Are you expressing love or hate, negative or positive, ego or God? It's your choice, what formula you wish to create.

In the immortal words of Jesus Christ:

"For happy are those who strive for peace, for they will find the peace of God. Give everyone your peace, even as I have given my peace unto you. May peace be with you."

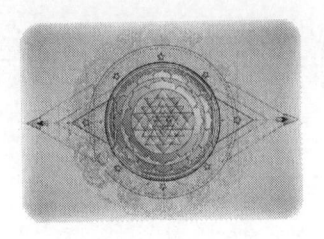

6

Divine Disciplines

Pranayama
BREATHING EXERCISES

Mind and body are connected by breath. It can be difficult to control the mind but we can easily regulate the breath. Prana (energy) yama (disciplines) is the Vedic name for breath exercises. The deeper the breath we take into our lungs fills them with oxygen (life force). Our lungs turn oxygen into Prana which is food for the nervous system (electricity) and nutrients for the blood. When we exhale (carbon dioxide) we eliminate waste and toxins. Therefore, being aware of the breath can offer more energy (life force) and cleanses the body of toxins. Pranayama also gives the mind a task, to watch the breath, this slows the minds wandering which distracts our concentration and meditation.

So Ham
Easy and comfortable

Long Breath
Inhale deeply / Exhale fully

1/4/2 Ratio
4 sec. inhale / 16 sec. retention / 8 sec. exhale

Hatha
Asana (posture or steady pose)

"Ha" (sun) "Tha" (moon)

Maintaining flexibility and strength increases circulation and provides nutrients and oxygen to the body. Hatha (asanas) are also concentration exercises to relax the body and to prepare it for silence and stillness. Performed slowly and consciously, as well as, focused on the breath, these exercises will produce physical effects and aid in concentration and meditation. Balancing masculine (right side of body/ sun) and feminine (left side/ moon) increases Prana (energy) which promotes higher consciousness (Kundalini).

YOGA ASANAS TO PRACTICE...

*Cat   Childs   Forward bend   Cobra   Corpse
Standing forward bend   Plow   Easy
Cow   Head to knee forward bend
Wide-angle forward bend*

Mantra
SACRED SOUND

(man-think) (thra-instrument) "Instrument of thought"

Words have tremendous power; they can arouse emotions and they can calm them. They direct, they infuriate, they reveal, they confuse; they are potent forces that bring up great reserves of strength, wisdom, and feelings.

In Yoga silence is practiced to discipline the tongue. The tongue is usually used as the destroyer and holding the tongue is the posture of the wise. Mantra is the tongue doing its greatest works. The first exercise for the tongue and mind is silence or sweet speech. Mantra (glories of the Lord) are purification techniques for the body, mind, atmosphere, food, and drink or all the elements; Fire, Air, Water, Earth and Space.

*Gayatri (Mother Mantra)
Omkar (Pranava)
Namasmarana (ever repetition of your Lords name)
Prayer and Song*

Gayatri
MOTHER MANTRA

The Gayatri is The Mother Mantra, the Universal prayer enshrined in the Vedas, the most ancient scriptures of man. It is addressed to the immanent (dwelling within) and the transcendent (beyond human experience) Divine which has been given the name "Savitha" (bright sun) meaning; that form which all this is born.

The Mantra consists of 24 powerful seed (bija) syllables invoking the Goddess Gayatri or Mother of the Universe. The Gayatri is repeated 3 times, 1st for praise, 2nd meditating on in reverence, 3rd prayer; an appeal is made to the Divine to awaken and strengthen the intellect of humanity.

"Om, Bhoor Bhuvaha Swaha
That Savitur Varenyam
Bhargo Devasya Dimahi
Dhiyo Yo Nah Prachodayath"

Om, O Divine Power, you who illumine the great sun and the three worlds of Earth, Air, and Heaven. We meditate upon the Divine radiance and we pray that you will illuminate our intellect to dispel our ignorance. The Mantra ends with; Om Shanti, Shanti, Shantihi (peace, peace, perfect peace).

The vibrations produced by this Mantra has been investigated to illumine the space around the chanter.

Omkar

21 OM Chant

Announcing the Lords presence

Omkar pays homage to the 20 Deities of the Body Temple; the 5 organs of action, the 5 organs of perception, the 5 vital airs, and the 5 sheaths of the body. This prepares the human being for mergence with the Supreme. The last OM (21) declares your Divinity.

OM (aum) is the sound of creation and announces the Lords presence. All is God and OM is activating it AS THE Cosmic Sound. Matter, every molecule of it is saturated with the Divine (prana). The originating point is the atom which gives rise to the molecule, and finally it forms matter which, in turn, brings into existing being. When reciting the OM every atom vibrates the light of God and it charges the body and aura (atmosphere) with powerful regenerative effects.

The sound of OM is; A-O-U-M, take a deep breath and while holding the teeth and lips slightly apart, permit the A sound to vibrate in the throat. Let the sound rise up and enter the space behind the tongue and the A sound changes to the O sound. Let the sound roll over the tongue, as the space between the lips becomes narrower and narrower, the sound again changes from the O sound to the U sound. Finally, with the meeting of the lips the sound vibrates as M, this vibration is felt in the mouth, lips and nose. The M sound gradually tapers off like a plane flying overhead and far into the distance as it merges into silence.

Namasmarana
Ever repeating or remembering the name of God

Today all elements of the world are polluted. This age (epic of time) is called the Kali Yuga and has become the age of impurity. The Vedas speak of 4 ages that make one "Maha Yuga" (great age). 1st age in Sanskrit (ancient language of the Vedas) is Kritha Yuga or Golden Age, 2nd is the Thretha Yuga or Silver Age, 3rd Dwapara Yuga or Bronze Age and 4th the Kali Yuga or Age of Steel. The Vedas prescribed certain behaviors of devotion for each Yuga. In Kritha it was Dhyana (meditation) and in the Thretha asceticism was prescribed. The Dwapara Yuga was the age of worship and the Kali Yuga is prescribed Namasmarana.

Repeating your beloved Lords name is powerful Shakti (creative energy). There are many names to choose from and any name will do, it is important to choose one you adore, the name and form will be useful for your concentration and devotion. God's name should be said with devotion and sweetness without desire or reward, this mantra is love and gratitude with contentment and praise. Virtuous character and adherence to the Divine message for our behavior are essential ingredients.

"OM SAI RAM"

Dhyana
Meditation and Concentration
One point mindedness

Dhyana is meditation, and to improve our meditation we must practice concentration (Dharana). 1 Dharana is 12 seconds of concentration. 1 Dhyana 12 seconds x 12 or 2 minutes and 24 seconds. 1 Dhyana x 12 equals 28 minutes and 48 seconds or Samadhi (equanimity) or calm mind and proves your mastery over mind. Once we master the mind meditation blossoms. The meditator considers realization of inner bliss important. Promotion of the welfare of the world is an equally important aim. To carry out this aim, we must bring certain physical, verbal, and mental tendencies under control. The physical tendencies are; injury to life, adulterous desire, and theft. The verbal sins are; false alarms, cruel speech, jealous talk and lies. The mental attitudes are; greed, envy, and the denial of God. The destruction of the modifications and agitations of the mind is prerequisite to obtaining audience with the Divine. His/her mansion has 8 doors through which one has to pass for an audience.

1. Control of the inner senses

2. Control of the outer senses

3. Disciplined posture

4. Regulated breath

5. Turning the mind inwards

6. Single mindedness

7. Meditation

8. Perfect equanimity

When the mind is cleaned of all sediment or impurity and noble feelings are cultivated then wisdoms vision can come out and creation is perceived in all its splendor.

Jyoti Meditation
Dhyanam (candle light meditation)

Light is the greatest purifier; it dispels all darkness. God is of the nature of effulgence, and light is thus the most appropriate symbol of Gods real nature. After seating oneself in a comfortable and steady posture, chant at least 3 Oms (preferably 21) to assist in calming and steadying the mind. Then steadying the breath, comfortable breath, gaze straight ahead at the candle flame. Look on the flame steadily for some time, then close your eyes, see and feel the flame inside you between your eyebrows. Let the flame slide down into the lotus of your heart, illuming the path. See the Jyoti (light) in the midst of the petals of the heart, which is conceived as a lotus flower, the petals of which will soon open. Watch the petals of the heart unfold one by one, bathing every thought, feeling, impulse, and emotion in the light, dissolving all shadows. There is no space for darkness to hide. It has to flee before the light. The light of the flame becomes wider and brighter. Let it pervade your limbs, now those limbs can never indulge in dark, suspicious, and wicked activities; they have become instruments of light and love. As the light reaches up to the tongue, falsehood vanishes from it. Let it rise up the eyes and ears destroying all dark desires that infest them. Let your head be surcharged with light all wicked thoughts will flee therefrom. Imagine that the light is in you more and more intensely; let it shine all around you, and let the light spread from you, in ever widening circles, taking in your loved ones, your friends, strangers and enemies, all men and women, all living beings, the entire world.

Meditation on the Form

First, when you sit for meditation, OM or repeat you Lords name to clear and calm the mind. Then gradually, while reciting your chosen name, draw before the mind's eye the form which that name represents. When your mind wanders away from the recital of the name, take it on the picture of the form. When it wanders away from the picture, lead it on the name. Tame and discipline the mind with this exercise. The imaginary picture you have drawn will get transmuted into the emotional picture, dear to the heart and fixed in the memory; gradually, it will become the "Sakshathkarachitra" when the Lord assumes that form in order to fulfill your desire.

Bhakti
Devotion / Worship / Service

The Sages (wise men) have described 9 ways of expressing devotion to God and attaining liberation. They are:

1. Keerthanam, singing the glories of God

2. Vishnusmaranam, ever remembering the Lord

3. Paadasevanam, worshiping the Lords feet

4. Vandanam, prostration

5. Daasyam, dedicated service

6. Sneham, friendliness

7. Archanam, offering daily worship

8. Atmanivedanam, total surrender

The particular form of God that one worships is less important than one's sincere devotion to the Divine. The essence of Bhakti is Love and not formal exercises or worship of various kinds, worship should be offered to the Divine who resides in all beings. Love is God, live in love. Love is the means of realizing bliss of the self, which is centered in ourselves, it need not be sought elsewhere. It can be found within one's self when all thoughts are controlled, and the mind is turned inwards. Dedicate all actions to the Lord. This is the highest knowledge. It is the Summum Bonum of existence.

SO-HAM "SO" on the inhale "HAM" exhaling

Meaning: I AM ONE (may be also chanted mentally)

✻

OM MANI PADME AUM

Hail the Jewel in the Lotus

✻

OM TA-RA TU-TA-RE TU-RE SO-HA

Tara, You Are the Guiding Star.

Prayers

Lord make me an instrument of your peace.
Where there is hatred, let me sow love.
Where there is injury, pardon.
Where there is doubt faith.
Where there is despair, hope.
Where there is darkness, light.
And where there is sadness, joy.
O Divine master, grant that I may not so much seek
To be consoled, as to console;
To be understood, as to understand;
To be loved, as to love;
For it is in giving that we receive.
It is in pardoning that we are pardoned;
And it is in dying that we are born to eternal life.

Beloved Lord, help me be, your perfect devotee,
teach me to love all things, and grant me sight to see.
The Universe is one with you, All is Divinity.
There is no "I", there is no "me", there isn't even "we",
there's only one, the Holy One, of blessed Divinity.
Beloved Lord, help me be, your perfect devotee,
be my food, be my drink, walk this life with me.
On the path to merge with you, detachment is the key,
when all of these, I have learned, forever will I be,
One with you, for all of time, the perfect devotee.

Shakti, your body is the world
the rivers are your veins,
and the forest, your hair.
The firmament is your dress,
the mind is your breath.
You are the pair of oppposites,
you are the past and present,
the soft and gentle,
the terrible and the fierce.
Your sounds are silence,
you are waves of sound,
and the power of silence.
You are the Human and the Divine,
you are elevated places,
the Labyrinth,
the One without a second.
O Mother of many aspects
We honor thee with great reverence
Om, Om, Om.

Songs

All I ask of you is forever to remember me
as loving you (X2)

Ishk Allah Mahebood Lillah (X2)
(Arabic for: God is love, lover, and beloved)

The name of God is flowing within me
I hear it always singing within me
ALLAH ALLAH SHIVAYA SHAKTI GOVINDA
RAMA RAMA JEHOVAH BUDDAH LORD JESUS

Divine Mother so-ham you and I are One
Siva Shakti so-ham you and I are One
Jesus Christ so-ham you and I are One
Divine Father so-ham you and I are One
Brahma Brahma so-ham you and I are One
Allah Allah so-ham you and I are One
Buddha Buddha so-ham you and I are One
Rama Sita so-ham you and I are One

Love Love Love Love
people we were made for Love
love each other as ourselves
for we are One

Bibliography

Macrobiotic Diet by Michio and Aveline Kushi

Magnetism and the Divine Professor by Lawrence W. Fagg

Magical Mind Magical Body by Deepak Chopra M.D.

Conversations with God (Books 1-3) by Neal Donald Walsch

Why People Don't Heal and How They Can by Carolyn Myss, Ph.D.

Energy Anatomy by Carolyn Myss, Ph.D.

A Letter to Karth by Elia Wise

Autobiography of A Yogi by Paramahansa Yogananda

Babaji and the 18 Siddah Kriya Yoga Tradition by Marshal Govindan

Hidden Messages in Water by Masaru Emoto

The Upanishads by Swami Prabhavananda and Frederick Manchester

Way of the Peaceful Warrior by Dan Millman

Advaita Vedanta by Eliot Deutsch

Vedanta Treatise by A. Parthasarathy

Beyond the Siddhis by John McAfee

Mutant Message Down Under by Mario Morgan

The Art of Peace by John Stevens

Greater Than You Know by Peter Phipps

Mary's Message to the World by Annie Kirkwood

Upanishad Vaahini by Bhagavan Sri Sathya Sai Baba

Spirit and Mind by Samuel H Sandweiss, M.D.

Pathways to God (Vols. 1 – 3) by Jonathan Roof

The Mysticism of Sound and Music by Inayat Khan

The Celestine Prophecy by James Redfield

You Are A Spiritual Being Having A Human Experience by Bob Frissell

Taming our Monkey Mind by Phyllis Crystal

Alkalize or Die by Dr. Theodore A. Baroody

The PH Miracle by Robert O. Young Ph.D. and Shelly Redford Young

Loving God by Professor by N. Kasturi

A Recipe for Bliss by Carl Schmidt

Reprograming Our Spiritual Sadhana by Indulal Shah

When God Walks the Earth by Jack Shemesh

Made in the USA
Columbia, SC
24 September 2021